IN WORDSWORTH'S CHAIR

For
Robert and Pamela Woof

Also by Gerard Benson

Name Game (1971)

This Poem Doesn't Rhyme (Editor, 1990)

Poems on the Underground
(Joint Editor, four editions, 1991, 1992, 1993, 1994)

The Magnificent Callisto (1992)

Does W Trouble You? (Editor, 1994)

Evidence of Elephants (1995)

for Ewa Kuniczsk

IN WORDSWORTH'S CHAIR

~~Gerard Benson~~

Gerard Benson
5 v 96

Cathy Ben
best wishes Ewa

FLAMBARD

in association with
THE WORDSWORTH TRUST

ACKNOWLEDGEMENTS

Some of these poems have appeared in the following publications:
Evidence of Elephants, How to be Well-Versed in Poetry, The Literary Review, The Page, Pivot, The Spectator.

The cover design is by Catherine Benson.

Flambard Press wishes to thank Northern Arts for its financial support.

Published in 1995 by Flambard Press
4 Mitchell Avenue, Jesmond, Newcastle upon Tyne NE2 3LA

Typeset by Stephen Hebron for The Wordsworth Trust, Grasmere, Cumbria
in association with Sally Woodhead
Printed in Great Britain by Cromwell Press, Broughton Gifford,
Melksham, Wiltshire

A CIP catalogue record for this book is available from the British Library
ISBN 1 873226 15 2
©Gerard Benson 1995

CONTENTS

DC MS 44	*7*
Grasmere Sonnet	*7*
Cumberland Wall	*8*
Campion	*10*
October Sonnet	*10*
Early Morning Walk	*11*
A Seal, An Eagle	*11*
Ravens	*12*
Dance of the Scarecrows	*13*
Photo-Call, Dove Cottage	*14*
On Greenhead Gill with Grasmere School	*15*
Alpine Fire	*16*
Becalmed	*17*
Fog Ice	*18*
Snow	*19*
You See the Spider	*20*
The Dark Gleam of Pitch	*21*
Burnt	*21*
Mobile	*22*
One Letter in an Alphabet Somewhere	*24*
As the Door Opened	*24*
Stick	*25*
Music at Night	*26*
Visitation	*27*
Diagnosis	*27*
And Again	*28*
Princess Enchanted	*29*
The Hat	*30*
Angels	*30*
Giraffe	*31*

The Little Animals

1	*Introduction*	*32*
2	*The Paper Beetle*	*33*
3	*The Cardboard Cat*	*34*
4	*The Papier Mâché Mouse*	*35*
5	*The Rubber Dog*	*36*
6	*The Wooden Horse*	*37*
7	*The Tin Ox*	*38*
8	*The Cloth Bird*	*39*
9	*The Cotton Bear*	*40*
10	*The Glass Wolf*	*41*

Two Riddles — *42*
Sonnet *(for Kit Wright)* — *43*
Unkissed Triolet — *43*
Kyrielle of a Thousand Kisses — *44*
D.I.Y. — *46*
A Thespian Rondeau — *46*
R.I.P. — *47*
My Midden — *47*
Inventory — *48*

DC MS 44

(A homemade vellum-bound notebook in which Dorothy and Mary Wordsworth copied Wordsworth's poems, for Coleridge to take with him to Malta, 1804; Dove Cottage manuscript collection)

Holding it in my hands, trying its weight,
The thick, small book, I feel a thump and throb
Of blood against my temples. The copied
Poems, page after page covered with deft, neat
Writing, *verso* and *recto*, detonate
Silently inside me, a time bomb
Fused by those women, in the slow, long
Days of labour, filling the homemade
Fascicles with glowing odes and sonnets – *There was*
A time . . . The world is too much with us . . . Nuns
Fret not (nor, it seems, sisters and wives,
The copyists): and more – set firm across
Their graceful loops, an uglier, darker hand,
Wordsworth's, correcting. This vellum enfolds lives.

GRASMERE SONNET

Robbed of my eyes by Wordsworth, I look down
On lake and landscape from Grey Crag. The sky
Is ponderous, the water still, and I
Half see it sullenly repeat the brown
Hillside (a foxy tan); a heron flown
To the island disappears among the high
Trees far below me; wisps of white cloud fly
Suddenly up beyond the ridge; the crown
Of a distant hill catches a shaft of light:
And, germinating under all, I sense
Wordsworth's erupting bones, which rouse to fight –
Ribs, dumb-bell thigh and spine – death's immanence;
And, shoving through that range off to my right,
The *os frontalis*, sober and immense.

CUMBERLAND WALL

Prehistoric,
this wall
between nothing
and nothing,
air and air,
that scrambles
crazily across
the hills,
not stopping
for outcrops
but staggering
on over them:
xylophone vertebrae,
skeleton of an
extinct beast,
mythological, even,
skinned dragon
of the crests
and valleys,
tottering on
through time and
distance, stone
on stone, poised
one on the other
by hands now bone
or dust, on and on
over rise, into dell;
lichened, mossed,
gappy, showing
wedges of sky;
fossil holding
fossils, as it
clings and stumbles
determinedly forging
a ramshackle way

over the green
hillsides, still
to be doing it
after the last
weapon has been
launched, the last
breath breathed,
the last promise
broken; perching
on humps of hill,
separating nothing
from nothing, air
from air, marking
a forgotten dogma,
treading stonily
among buttercups;
shackling the slopes
where raven
and buzzard quarrel,
where skylarks swoop;
heavy necklace
of grey rocks
adorning the marshy
fields and daisy
constellations, strung
out to the sky edge.

CAMPION

Black splodges blotch the leaves. Trees arch the lane,
Huge above moss and nettles. Lank and dying
The foliage of a fallen foxglove's lying
Slack over ivy. The wall is overgrown
With green, root, fern; though here and there a stone
Shows, bulbous, massive, prehistoric, saying,
'I am here. Was set here. And here I'm staying
Till the trees have fallen and the lane has gone.'
Another year has come to late September,
Yet still cow parsley stands, yellowing, tall.
The land is changing colour. Autumn showers
Have sharpened up the fields. I shall remember
This lane, this pinching wind, this wall,
This verge, dark green, but starred with purple flowers.

OCTOBER SONNET

The trees are stripping down again, to show
(Quaint exhibitionists) their skeletons;
They wore pale green, then darker green, and now
It is their showiest garments they've put on,
Orange and red and yellow, for the wind
With soft importunate fingers to unpeel
With gentle skill, and carry to the ground,
Or in a sudden wild access of zeal
Tear off and brandish to the sky. This is
No nightclub frolic or slow, teasing dance,
No roguish play with colours and the breeze.
The season, now, with neat mortician's hands,
Has touched the outer clothing of the trees,
And will, in time, display their weathered bones.

EARLY MORNING WALK

With florid ingenuity, the designer of fungus
Has been at it again. All along the ditch
They poke out like lumps of yeast rising, or fingers,
Or pixie parasols, to poison the writers of kiddie kitsch.
You find them peculiarly glued to beech boles like shelves,
Or among roots, or standing in perfect circles, the fungi;
Or squatting, little smoking balls, in glades and dells,
On days when mists invade and the air is tangy.
Although their autumnal spectrum is mostly muted,
It is enlivened from time to time with spectacular reds.
These silentest of beings must certainly be bruited
In loud voices for the sudden way they show their heads.
  The designer has again been displaying his precocity;
  You have to admire his verve, his insidious virtuosity.

A SEAL, AN EAGLE

The lake is a cold mirror, steely, truthful,
In which a grove of trees hangs upside down.
A skiff. The whispers of lovers. Flare of a match.

I watch from Whindle Crag, imagining I am a seal
Swimming where the planet's reflection shivers,
Until a cloud erases the starlight
And inks over the trees in the lake.

The crag darkens. I imagine an eagle.
And the lovers, each the other's mirror,
Flare into invisible flame.

RAVENS

They waddle with clipped wings,
Glossy and sleek as aldermen,
At the Tower, where they draw their pensions.

Glutted with the queen's silver shilling,
Tamed sycophants, fed every day,
They serve their time in pomp and luxury.

But above Great Rigg the ravens
Plunge the air; dangerous against the sky
They tumble sideways and cry

Out in guttural talk; they roll against heaven's
Cloudy blue, wheeling, flipping and banking,
Loud-voiced adventurers, high over the mountain,

Who dare everything. Slapped by the wind, they soar
And descend; forage in all seasons – cold
Rain, sleet, or roasting sun – they hunt, caracole

On flexing wings and rasp their rough words. They war
With buzzards. And when all is finished, leave dark
Feathers and pale bones to decorate the crag.

DANCE OF THE SCARECROWS

Arms lifted sideways
Each guards a furrow.
It is a dance of possession.
They are ranged across the field
Like chess men.

Balanced on one foot
They grandly gesture,
A choreography of rags,
Whisking to the wind's music
On bare brown earth.

Since people began
To tame the fields
This outdoor ballet
Has played in all weathers
To its audience of earth and sky.

The dancers' mouths are dumb.
But a couple of sticks,
An old green dress, a torn
Jacket, a dead man's hat
Leap to the land's rhythm.

PHOTO-CALL, DOVE COTTAGE

Sitting in Wordsworth's chair to have my photo taken
I am uneasy in the preposterousness of my position,

As if the chair itself (which bears a plaque) had conferred
On it some especial charisma by the bum of the bard,

Or there were some impiety in thus posing
With a thoughtful look, enhanced by my half-moon glasses

(No longer NHS unfortunately) beside this pile
Of manuscripts which I am not currently reading, but will

Certainly read in the fairly near future. 'Pensive'
Might well be more appropriate than 'thoughtful', above,

To describe the grimace of one who sits in this oddly-shaped chair
Beside this window, in this part of Grasmere,

I am now thinking, ever the ironist. But it will, I can't help
Supposing, have been different for Wordsworth himself.

The chair, though, is comfortable, the view terrific, and any
Minute now a mighty Ode will (possibly) come pouring from my pen.

And I shall be delighted, I willingly confess,
If ever I see the resulting picture in the local press.

ON GREENHEAD GILL
WITH GRASMERE SCHOOL

Ice hung from the bridge;
It made an arched hall,
A beast's mouth some said,
Or the Ice Queen's realm.

We went through a dark cave;
We held a rope rough in the hands.
We sang a song
And heard the cave's dark sound.

Out in the light we climbed
To the top of a high hill;
We sat on grey rocks
To eat our lunch.

The sun shone. The ice shone.
The grass shone. The rocks shone.
Ice grew in spikes.
Ice sheathed the roots.

It was a day to hoard in the mind,
So I write some of it down,
In short words, sharp, clear,
To match the day.

ALPINE FIRE

Flames flicker on the snowy hillside.
The grate is diamonded with icicles.

It is as though strawberries packed in ice
Were delivered in a cellophane wrapper,
Inexplicably to our cabin,
The gift of an unnamed stranger.

Or as though intense blue eyes
Had been watching through a window
Or through jewelled binoculars
While we walked together . . .

As though fossilised tyre tracks
Glinted in the snow, near where we had wandered
(Though no vehicle was ever seen)
And brought imagined fire to this white winter.

There are flames in the snow.
And, hanging in the grate
As the logs are devoured,
Slim icicles glistening and white.

BECALMED

Masts, rigging and tackle
of abandoned vessels –
the dark trees, leafless,
ride the stony waves
that crop out of these hills,
their dangling sails
useless rags of mist.

Inked onto damp paper
this landscape offers puzzles
of perception – clouds which loop
in disconsolate curves,
mountains whose contours
stay subtly veiled.
Nothing is definite.

There is no wind.
The grey moisture is draped
motionless round the crags,
erasing their edges;
and closer, the ghost ships
ride at anchor
on the hard, still sea.

FOG ICE

The thousand leaves of the bushes
Are thorned with ice.
Minute splinters
Serry the leaf edges,
Sharp, gleaming, like barbaric

Jewellery, intricately bright.
Every stem white;
Each branch brilliant,
Drawn upcurving against
Dark houses, the loaded sky.

Grace and beauty – silversmith's work,
But cold as fear.
Filigree ferns,
Tall beeches are sugared
Sculpture. Tiny glass daggers

Protect rose petals; oaks display
Their skeletons,
White in the murk.
Words float in the chill air,
Writhing shapes of mist in mist.

SNOW

Another snow poem:
White falls onto white,
Loading the landscape.

Contours vanish.
Boundaries cease to exist.
The white is intolerable:

Reams of emptiness,
A wedding gown,
A chill anaesthetic.

In galloping metres
The hare, the stoat
Print snow poetry.

Firs are weighted with white.
Skeletal birches bend
Under their cold burden.

Fooling in the snow, once,
My breath condensed
And my beard crisped,

Frozen in hundreds
Of tiny icicles.
Today it is indoors

I play with snow,
Watching through glass
As earth and sky fill up.

YOU SEE THE SPIDER

You see the spider legging it upward
Into the rose leaf's dark shadow,
And notice silken filaments, which swing
In the not quite still air.

This evening the facade is floodlit,
An unpleasant metallic yellow,
And seen so, the rose bush by the lounge
Bar window is a lure for night insects.

Where they stumble and fly, an army of spiders
Prepares to greet them, weaving
Busy welcomes; little severed hands
Which twitch below moulting flower heads,

Small disembodied finger joints
Gathering and scratching, twisting silk,
While behind the glass the bar-room talk,
Oblivious to these silent events, winds on.

Yes. They are certainly like hands, tiny,
Purposeful, independent, dextrous; you note
That only a transparent wall separates
The hands from those who chat within.

THE DARK GLEAM OF PITCH

From the very centre of its blackness,
Pitch gleams, as though within its heart
It held the jewel of light. So it is
In the darkest passages of our love –
An interior radiance streams from the shadows,
As if all darkness were an abstraction,
An enigma to be pondered only,
A paradox to be debated, not credited.

It is hard to believe that there is no
Blind spot at the centre of the diamond.
How else does carbon radiate an iridescent dance
So savage that the mind, as well as the eye,
Is dazzled? Such an excess of light demands
A kernel of darkness in which knowledge may germinate.
For as much as from emotion, from understanding
Grows love with all its extravagant paraphernalia.

BURNT

You burned me with your kisses,
And I felt cold within;
As if desire had frozen
My heart onto my skin.

MOBILE

I wake up on Saturday morning
Expecting to find you there, but you have gone.

There's no note on the kitchen table.
I wonder if I'll ever see you again.

I walk down to the cliff and look at the sea.
The tide is in, but it seems quite changed,

Tired; the water is a washed-out green.
All around, companies of gulls are wheeling;

In desolate voices they are crying.
Cattle in the fields briefly lift their heads

But they're unconcerned by my passing
And return to their feeding. I imagine

Where you may be and walk back via the lane.
A woman driving a tractor greets me

But her heart is not in it. I see
Chaffinches and seriously consider

Renaming them but give up the idea.
I return home and make myself coffee.

It tastes like nothing. I search the house and find
An unknown sock. I shrug. I shave. I catch

My reflection in the bathroom mirror.
And the phone does not ring. I strip the sheets.

I bash the pillows flat. I open the window.
The clock has stopped. When did you leave?

On the wardrobe floor I find one hooked ear-ring,
Pale blue, mathematical, a nest

Of interlaced free-moving shapes. I attach
A thread to the hook, a pale blue thread,

And pin it to the wardrobe ceiling
Firmly with a white drawing pin.

ONE LETTER IN AN ALPHABET SOMEWHERE

You can see the only
Possible tap pouring endlessly
Into the desert, and you try

To call out, but the words
Are distorted and you find
You are calling the name

Of a lost love, although
On waking you cannot remember
Anything more than a perfume;

But there is one letter
In an alphabet somewhere
Which might be used to spell

The name you are seeking,
Though your chances of discovering it
Are, at best, minimal.

AS THE DOOR OPENED

they moved apart
like seaweeds

separated by a shift
in the current,

and colour drained
from the space between them.

STICK

I tap pavements and tickle walls.

I am a leader. People take notice of me.
I tap tap through crowds.

I find kerbs and edges, and all for her.
She holds me delicately, folds me
To hide me in the dreadful darkness
Of her pocket. I do not blame her.

What can she know of darkness,
Who knows no light? Tap, tap.

I serve her better than the dog
Although she speaks to it and gives it a name.
Tap, tap. Tap, tap.

Vertiginous the days when I slowly swish
From side to side, moving forward
Into the dark nothing. Dull
The folded pocket days. Tap, tap.

I must be going now.

Tap tap. Tap tap.
Tap tap.

MUSIC AT NIGHT

On Second Avenue the traffic
Makes unsweet music.
In rasping counterpoint
A staccato blurting
Of horns pummels the night,

Fearsome jabs of sound
Till one, then another
And at last a third
Cry out together
In a thumb-jammed howl.

Florid sirens hurl
Sudden spirals of sound,
Looped scraps of discord,
Weird whistlings
And crazed shrieking.

Hurrying cargoes clatter
Endlessly past this window.
Klaxons high and low,
Like disputing birds,
Call and reply.

Shop fronts dazzle
The wet sidewalks.
The shifting of gears never ceases,
Nor tyre swish,
Nor the growl and grumble of motors.

At 2 a.m. the hoarse
Untuneful voice of a man singing,
As he walks slowly homeward
(No words recognisable), echoes
Not unlike beauty, among the din.

VISITATION

Last night a new dragon came.
It crawled up from terrible depths.
Some crevice far down in the brain
Was its home, but it had left that cave
Meaning to seek me out and speak to me.
Its voice was ill-equipped for human converse.
Pitiful it was to hear its rasped attempts,
As though words hurt its crocodilian throat.

What was it that that monster tried to say
With so much pain and difficulty? And in what
Forgotten tongue? Advice? A threat? A warning?
Wingless it lumped along across a soft terrain,
Grunting brief phrases in an obsolete language,
And looked about from grey, unlidded eyes.

DIAGNOSIS

Bout Rimés

You build with fragments of my shattered hope
As shrinks assemble random images
(A star, a bayonet, an antelope)
A suite of unlocked rooms, claiming that these
Once occupied will make me less alone.
But that is not my problem. I'm beset
With angry ghosts. If I were carved from stone
Then some escape were possible. To get
This mess into some shape, I need austere
Aloneness. Then my foes in single file
Would silently retreat, and without fear
I'd face the chaos, even, perhaps, smile.

AND AGAIN

And again the impression
That this second would always be remembered:
The palings, the groundsel, ragwort on the bombsite,
The footpath across the rubble,
The sky, the panting mongrel.

The air itself felt unfamiliar. The house
Stood vivid on the embankment,
Its edges drawn in sharp pencil lines.
Voices, distinct, from the recreation ground
A mile away, carried on the warm air.

As a child she had looked once
Into her grandfather's spectacles, while the old man
Was quietly talking perhaps (how could she be sure?)
Of some matter in one of the books
In the glass bookcase behind her.

Seeing reflected in the lenses
The reflecting glass of the bookcase
Reflecting a tiny window (the same that lay
Behind the old man's head) had given her
A piercing moment of hypnotic enchantment.

PRINCESS ENCHANTED

Lifting under wing wind,
In a pliancy of bone
I dance on air,

And sing my curling
Plainsong in the monasteries
Of rock that castle the shore,

Where you walk, as I
In heavy dresses of brocade
Walked once. Such wizardry

Is worked in the caves
Or earth-edge, sea-lip,
That now a bird (for what

Forgivable offence I choose
Not to remember)
I sweep, wind held

Air hurled, spinning
My minuet, feathered
White and grey, compelled

To tread the gusting breeze
Till all worlds have ended
And all spells died.

THE HAT

To cover the nakedness of my mother's eyes
A small black veil hung from her hat.
Sheer gloves sheathed her arms to the elbows.

Such a dotty little hat, quite Myrna Loy,
She said, pouring tea from a silver pot.
In Swan & Edgar's tea room,
Her laughter tinkled like a teaspoon.
A ducky little hat, don't you think?

The veil moved in the wind of her breath.
The hat perched on her curls, a small black box.
There were no fingers to the gloves,
And she fed triangles of honeyed toast
Into the awful space behind the veil.

ANGELS

Someone has bolted three angels
To the southern wall,
Flattened them and spread them
Splay-winged against stone,
With rivets through their plumage.
Facing northward for eternity
(Or while this dark cathedral stands)
They gleam yellow with reflected light.

Like crucified eagles they hang
With the placid faces of choirboys.
What was their offence?
Surely they are blameless.
And who is it who dares daily to scour
Their lifted wings, their beautiful faces,
Here in this ornate prison
Where all but they may come and go?

GIRAFFE

*'The Admirablest and Fairest Beast
that I Euer Saw, was a Iarraff.'*
(17th Century Pilgrim)

Swaying just a little, he strolls
Aloofly among the gazelles
Clothed in a golden net
But this is no swaggerer.
Never more than seven miles
From water, he treads
Fastidiously on tough hooves
Like a slow hallucination,
Or like the oblique
Foot-certain moves,
Lissom on booted feet,
Of a lanky lightweight;
Or like a loose-jointed dancer,
Rehearsing new steps.
The air buckles in the heat
Distorting his long shape.
His gallop is quick but gawky,
A rangy teenager among
infants.
He travels under aliases,
Zarapha, Orafle, Gerfaunt;
Ziraph too (almost angel
But he wears stubby horns
And chews as he stares about),
Silently surveying
From languid film-star eyes
The acres that surround him.

THE LITTLE ANIMALS

Poems for 'Próle do Bébé, Nº 2' by Villa-Lobos

1 *Introduction*

On shelf and bed and floor,
Or stuffed in bags or boxes,
They rest, the toys – just things
Of wood or cloth or paper,
Simply lifeless shapes,
Till, woken from their slumber,
They are given a living soul
By a child's imagination.
Then cat and dog and mouse and horse,
Beetle, ox and bear and bird,
Become themselves. And, listen:
The wolf's clear howl is heard.

2 *The Paper Beetle*

By the bed's foot
Where it has fallen,
There lies a beetle;
Curved, and fashioned
From brightly coloured paper:
Head, thorax
And six, angular legs.

It is so still you might suppose it dead;
But listen to the song inside its head.

Paper beetle a paper beetle
I scuttle onward, forever onward,
And hurry forward, over grasses,
I'm up a seedling and down another.
I'm always moving. I'm never stopping,
Across the grass which is splashed with sunlight
And barred with shadow. I dodge the spider.
I just keep crawling with all my legs and I
Scuttle on and I scuttle on.
Through leaves and petals, until I fall, of course.
If I fall I shall wave my legs until,
Wave my legs until, wave my legs until,
Wave my legs until, wave my legs until
Something happens and I'll scurry on,
Then I'll hurry on. Then I'll hurry on.

3 *The Cardboard Cat*

Pussy, Pussy, cut from cardboard,
On the top shelf of the cupboard,
Black of whisker, striped tail pointed,
By a small brass rivet jointed,
Stares from painted eyes, unwinking,
Never shows what she is thinking:
　　In the jungle of her thoughts.

But if you knew her thinking,
You would imagine slinking,
Peering round corners, blinking
　　　　While she
　　Sized up her prey.
You would see supple stalking
Graceful and dangerous walking;
And if you heard her talking
　　　　This is
　　What you'd hear her say:

Mgnaaoourr! Mgnaaaoourrr!

4 *The Papier Mâché Mouse*

Mouse is a twitch,
Is a whisker,
Is a skittering run,
Is a shiny eye,
Is a wrinkling snitch;
Is a cheesy nibbler,
Is a big-eared inquisitive skedaddler.

Tell no cat about this mouse.
Tell no trap-minded murderer.
Tell no worrisome terrier.

Let it sit on the pillow,
Wearing its little bow-tie.
Let it squeak its little song.

And when night comes,
Let it dream
Of green cheese hills
On a thin slice of moon.

5 *The Rubber Dog*

I was made in a mould, like all the others;
I have many identical brothers.
We wear our logos on a front pad.
I am not really sad,
It's just the way my eyes
Were painted on. I'm quite glad
To be with a family; though the boy tries
To twist my tail off. It'll spring
Back, but it's a nasty feeling.
And the girl drops me downs-
tairs to watch which way I'll bounce.
Oh well . . .
I just pick myself up,
Like any young pup . . .
And mosey back to my kennel.
Good to be home.
I grab and worry my nice rubber bone.

6 The Wooden Horse

Ridden by fingers, which dance him
   Over a scrubbed pine floor,
He gallops on stiff straight legs
   Till he comes to the huge cliff door.
His nostrils are perfectly carved,
   Also his billowing mane;
He trots back across the room
   To the forest of chairs again.

Trotting on, trotting on, trotting on!
   Galloping, galloping, galloping!
His rider stays with him as he leaps
   With a tremendous spring
Onto the perilous plateau land
   On top of the nursery table;
Then one last crazy canter round
   And back to the toybox stable.

7 *The Tin Ox*

Hoof after hoof he gravely places,
Swinging his heavy head before him,
Pushing against the yoke that holds his
    Shoulders back.
Dragging the heavy plough behind him,
Down on the long brown rug you see him,
Patiently plodding onward plodding
    To the fringe.

His mind is dark as the shed without windows
Where he spends his resting hours.
He is a monument to mild endurance,
Warm-blooded servant, uncomplaining,
A tin ox with curved horns, who turns at the rug's edge
And begins, treading forward on split hoofs,
The slow parallel return journey.

The child who plays with the ox is patient, too;
By bedtime the rug will be neatly furrowed,
Like corduroy.

8 *The Cloth Bird*

The cloth bird hangs by the window
   On a length of string,
And all the birds in the garden
   Visit her and sing.

She hangs quite still in the window,
   Motionless for hours –
A warbler of white linen,
   Covered with blue flowers.

Then a breath of wind will move her,
   Rock her here and there –
But all the birds in the garden
   Are free as the air.

The cloth bird is silent.
   She has no tongue.
But all the birds in the garden
   Fill the air with song.

They load the air with music:
   Twittering, cheeping, trilling,
Pink-a-pink, Cheeve-a-chee –
   Music so thrilling.

The cloth bird listens
   While the garden birds sing –
Hanging by the window
   On a piece of string.

9 *The Cotton Bear*

We have a pinkish cotton bear.
His eyes are buttons and they stare.
He wears a hat to hide his hair.
(You've never seen a bear with hair?
You've never seen our cotton bear.)

Our cotton bear's a dancing bear.
He frisks and frolics everywhere.
You leave him here, you find him there.
For instance, leave him on a chair,
You'll find him on the bottom stair;
Though if you leave him on the stair,
You'll find him on your bed, that's where.
He is an aggravating bear.

Then, sometimes, like a forest bear
He can be fierce, and then your hair
Would stand on end, to see him stare,
Or hear him growl. You would not dare
To quarrel with our cotton bear.
I'm very sure I would not care
To try, for like a grizzly bear,
He's at his fiercest in his lair
(Whether on shelf or box or chair
Or where he's chucked by Aunty Claire)
And then there's nothing that can scare
Our gallant pinkish cotton bear.

But mostly he is pretty fair.
He likes to sing a bearish air
Or dance the bear-dance, debonair,
Or simply sleep, our cotton bear.

10 *The Glass Wolf*

A glass wolf howls to a moon of glass.
He lopes on the clean white cloth
Through a forest where everything shines.

The tree trunks are transparent rods;
The fallen leaves that litter the earth
Are small splinters of dazzling crystal.

Wild wolf waif of glistening glass,
Tail low, back braced, his melody shivers the sky
(Starred ceiling of midnight blue).

To be so full of brittle glory!
To be forged of twisted glass
Held still by an inner force!

Fragile and fierce he turns up his head
And sings his long slow phrase
Fortissimo to the silent bulb of moon.

Like snow, like white icicles on the spine,
His voice. When you have heard this
You have heard the music of the wolf.

TWO RIDDLES

1

A strange vehicle I saw.
Two wheels turned on their axles
While a dead man spoke.

Numbers crawled on and on.
He who rode the vehicle
Sat on a swivelling chair.

He silenced the ghost
With a touch of his finger,
And prodded him to speak again.

2

I saw a white snake
Leave its tunnel
To lie on a bed of spikes
And enter a man's mouth,
Making him spit and froth.

Yet it was he
Who opened his lips
To receive the snake.

SONNET

for Kit Wright

Sometimes I write the last line first: 'a cheat',
I have been told; a poem ought to be
A quest, a journey of discovery,
A search for the heart's dark truth, not a mere feat
Of verbal conjuring. Quite true. But sweet
Encounters with eternal verity
Can come about through serendipity
As well as earnest strife; a sharp conceit
May speak as loud as any slaved-for truth.
So, while I move toward my chosen end,
Often, a barely understood idea will thrust
Itself onto the page, raw and uncouth,
As if some other self had steered my hand,
Although I sometimes write the last line first.

UNKISSED TRIOLET

I stood by the old kissing gate
But nobody kissed me.
Till nearly a quarter to eight
I stood by the old kissing gate.
There was Lily, Ramona and Kate;
How could they resist me?
I stood by the old kissing gate
And nobody kissed me.

KYRIELLE OF A THOUSAND KISSES

Da mi basia mille, deinde centum,
Dein mille altera, dein secunda centum,
Deinde usque altera mille, deinde centum.
Gaius Catullus

Fie, Love. The thing that we would do,
Catullus and his Lesbia knew;
Come to my waiting arms, sweet Lily:
  Da mi basia mille.

For, if Catullus knew his stuff,
A thousand kisses aren't enough,
So I implore you, willy-nilly:
  Da mi basia mille.

Lovers since Eden's time, I wist,
Have toyed and flirted, touched and kissed,
From Tonga to the Isle of Scilly:
  Da mi basia mille.

And nowadays it's often said
Under the neons green and red
That so enliven Piccadilly:
  Da mi basia mille.

At all the best Hunt Balls, you know,
One hears the cry, 'Yoicks! Tally-ho!
Come over here, you gorgeous filly:
  Da mi basia mille.'

It must, of course, remain in doubt
Whether Victoria would shout
To Brown, her ever-faithful ghillie:
  Da mi basia mille.

Yet sure I am that Abelard
And Eloise (whose fate was hard)
Whispered, although the night grew chilly:
   Da mi basia mille.

And Irish tenors too, I ween,
Have murmured to a fair colleen
Oft, in the night that Moore called 'stilly':
   Da mi basia mille.

At the *Moulin*, proud English earls
Have thus persuaded can-can girls
In frothing undies, wild and frilly:
   Da mi basia mille.

So we, my love, our supper done,
May now enjoy some Roman fun,
In spite of onions and Caerphilly:
   Da mi basia mille.

D.I.Y.

That's my last Turner, hanging on the wall,
Looking, my friend, I'm sure you will agree,
Quite the real thing; the treatment of the sea,
Lashed into turmoil by a sudden squall,
The light, the bending mast, the gulls, are all
My own unaided work, save that the key
Lies hidden underneath in numbers. 'Three'
(To take a case) signifies puce (that small
Tube there) and 'Nineteen' – that's gamboge. I call
This piece a marvel; so does Liz. Feel free
To look awhile, then join us through the hall
For home-made scones. (Next week I shall instal
A hatch.) And will you take some China tea,
Grown in the garden under glass, by me?

A THESPIAN RONDEAU

King Lear, V. iii. 271

'Edmond is dead, my lord' – that was my line
(In *King Lear*, Stratford, 1949).
Although I didn't have to learn a lot,
The line is quite important to the plot,
And Larry told me I was 'just divine'.

I was First Messenger; made the part mine.
In tights and jerkin, suavely saturnine,
I gave my reading everything I'd got:
    'Edmond is dead, my lord.'

I'd have preferred a line more sapphirine –
'The multitudinous seas incarnadine'
Rolls on the tongue (that's from the 'nameless Scot').
But still I thank the Lord above for what
He once allowed: a draught of vintage wine,
    'Edmond is dead, my lord!'

R.I.P.

Poor Tom lay dying. Faithful at his side
His wife and helpmeet sat, a tireless nurse,
Fixing his dosage, watching, anxious-eyed,
His laboured breathing sink from bad to worse,
Wiping his fevered forehead. He, poor soul,
With aching conscience, tried in vain to pray;
Then hot, remorseful tears began to roll
Across his cheeks. 'There's something I must say:
I have deceived you, Peg my dear,' he said,
'With cousin Beattie and your sister Joan.
I've lain with both, here in this very bed.'
'Don't fret, my love,' his wife replied. 'I've known
For years.' He stared. 'You knew?' 'Of course I knew.
Why else, dear Tom, would I have poisoned you?'

MY MIDDEN

I've a hidden midden in my garden,
Not a bad 'un, quite a good 'un,
Built by General Gordon for the poet Dryden
(Or was it Baden-Powell for Auden?),
Not a leaden midden, like they have in Sweden
(And in Baden-Baden),
But a wooden, such as are made in Jordan
(Or is it Arden? Beg your pardon!).

When the berries redden, branches harden,
And deadened leaves get damply trodden,
I put a cordon round my midden, with a warden.
It's forbidden then to man or maiden,
For it gets so sodden,
Laden with its sudden extra burden.
Yet in springtime all are bidden to my midden
Their saddened hearts to gladden,
For then my wooden garden midden is a very Eden.

INVENTORY

A telescope, a telephone,
Some ancient artefacts of stone,
A tiny black-and-white TV,
Will Shakespeare's works, the OED,
(And a few hundred other books);
Several small mugs that hang on hooks,
Some artificial flowers, a gamp,
An imitation antique lamp,
Two easy chairs, two upright ditto,
A table for these last to sit to;
Enough of knives and spoons and forks,
A radio that rarely works;
A tottering pile of magazines,
Some walking clothes (real stuff, not jeans),
Some OS maps, a Scrabble set,
Chessmen, a filing cabinet,
A typewriter; some plants, in pot.
These are the Grasmere goods I've got.

31 December 1994